The Harrowing Misadventures Of Life

Elizabeth Butler

BookLeaf Publishing

Presentation by *BookLeaf Publishing*

Web: www.bookleafpub.com

E-mail: info@bookleafpub.com

ISBN: 9789357210560

First edition 2022

DEDICATION

To my family for always being here and never doubting me.

ACKNOWLEDGEMENT

I would like to express my special thanks of gratitude towards to Writing On The Wall and the Write to Work scheme as I have gained confidence when writing and teaching me many new skills.

I would also like to thank Edge Hill University and the Creative Writing/ TV and Film tutors for pushing me to do the best I can possibly do.

PREFACE

The aim of this collection of poetry is to explore the lives of strangers through their mind, to show how the mind thinks. How normal life can turn unexpectedly dark.

Alone

We treasure those moments when we are left alone.
Left inside the house, left to your own devices,
The trouble comes when you are left with your own thoughts.
You may be surrounded by people, voices jumping out in every direction,
But the mind can be a dangerous place.
The thoughts can niggle their way through a good time, stop you in your tracks,
Reminding you that people are with you presently, but everyone is alone within their mind.
The suspicions and doubts try to worm their way into your brain,
Mushing all possible reasoning,
Juicy minds seem the best to control, fleshy skin and untamed minds ready to mould.
The most delectable is always the vulnerable.
Once was strong, know rotting from decay.
When we are both alone together, I can burry deep inside,
I will tighten your screams as they try and let loose.
You can try to beg, you can try to ask for assistances,

But truly,
we both know,
I am the only one for you.
Signed,
ALONE.

Echo

An Echo,
The constant ticking of something repeating,
Bang, Bang, Bang,
Drip, Drip drip.
The motion circling back around,
Newton's Cradle swishing back and forth.
An Echo,
Perhaps just an afterthought,
following the thing before,
a follower in the crowd.
The sounds caused by the reflection of waves,
arriving back in time.
The room echoes with the sound of its own
screams.
Bouncing back around.
A parallel of that feeling found in an echo,
That has repeated after the original has finished,
just like a copycat.
A reminder of that thing that once now no more.

FALL

Speeding down

Not being able to see my life in motion

the Sky,

the wind gushing

around my body,

my heart pounding

just like a drum

As I breathe,

my lungs finding it harder,

my head starts to gush,

dropping

dropping

dropping

and then
Just the feeling of being still
like I am flying on top of a lake
My body still feels as though
it is falling
but it's different,
it's less
Rapid.

I begin to float,
with more ease,
more at peace,
I touch the tips of the clouds with my
fingers,
it resembles that of calm water,
I was just
falling
in a wind-swept sea,
but
even though
I am falling,
I fall steadily,
a chance to catch a
glimpse
at the world below, the world becoming closer as
I drift though the skies,
just floating.

Where I land with a

THUMP.
My mind falling back down to reality.

Control

28 - Control

The first thing I see is the darkness,
Even when I open my eyes wide.
Before the boredom creeps in,
The light above is seen,
A heavily light.
The atmosphere changes,
I am no longer unable to see.
The room I find myself in doesn't provide much light,
But it better than where I was trapped inside.
My eyes crane, staring to the side.
An old wooden chest that is bolted from the outside.
I sigh, taking in my surroundings.
The place reminds me of a changing room,
Posters hang from dry walls,
Nic Nacs from long ago scattered around the place,
Feathers and notes flying around.
An old open wardrobe,
Showing a full suit top and tail.
Bright lights in the corner blind my tiny eyes,

A dozen bulbs lighting up the room around one smudgy mirror.
Underneath, a desk,
No, a dressing table!
My guess was correct.
Clothes drape from the top of the mirror,
Falling to the ground.
Makeup of many lying around.
Powder puffs in compacts, lipstick, and rouge.
I look up, gazing at the being above.
A woman,
Dressed formally, her suit and bow tie reflecting in front of her.
She grabs a top hat from the messy table holding me up to her face.
"This is it."
She tells me, taking one deep breath in.
In the moment we start to walk,
My body in contact with her palm.
The atmosphere turns much darker,
The sounds around us become more amplified,
The sounds of chatter and gossip.
From the little I can see,
We are standing in front of a closed curtain
When slowly they begin to depart from each other,
They reveal a crowd that cheers and claps,
I jingle around in her hand as she steps in front,
Taking a bow.

To the side,
A paper set, just like the one we are standing on,
But a much smaller scale.
I am placed in front,
Standing on paper wood.
Strings start to fly from my body,
I didn't know I even had.
I feel a yank from my back,
The joints in my legs and arms feel under control.
I stare up at the woman being,
She has my strings wrapped around her fingers.
Without any time to question,
I begin to move from side to side
This feel is odd?
I am not in control of my ligaments?
The strange, being above,
That who is in control of me now.

DARK

I was created before anyone else. A lone soul drifting around.
My partner soon followed, together things are born.
The irrational fear of me that you have astounds me.
I do not hurt, or touch you, how much damage can I do, really?
You are apprehensive because you just don't know me,
the unknown scares you, not the presence of me being with you.
Is that why you always choose my partner over me?
I made life,
I was the first
You have no right to say I shouldn't exist just to make your life less scary.
Many creatures love me,
they can't get enough of me.
Bats, Aye Aye, moles who always see my presence.
I complain,

but there are many of you who truly bask in my glory.
I am the only thing you see, even when you are awake.
A strange friend, always there.
The fact I am here with you, doesn't make your dreams more frightening,
try to tell yourself it's not me, it's you!
You are the only one capable to imagine your fears.
I feel like,
if you truly listen to your heart and mind, I am not the enemy here,
In fact, I shield you from danger.
I am excellent when you want to be concealed,
hiding your emotions from others,
Romantically, when you watch and kiss,
I will always be your wing man.
I may look scary, but the more you get to know me,
I'm a friend, a friend called darkness.

FLAME

The first thing I notice is the smell,
putrid, foul smelling
Like leather in a factory.
The smoke rises up
The grey fumes building up around me.
The flames burst into light of oranges, yellows, and reds,
my eyes stunned by its brightness.
I cough vigorously,
the dark foggy smoke bunches up inside my throat,
making it difficult to even breathe.
The colours, they dance in front of me,
like ballerinas at a concert.
I can feel myself drifting,
Once I could distinguish features,
now only bouncing flames.
I am overwhelmed by the sound,
crackling under foot, just like leaves in autumn.
Crack, pop!
The wood I had been resting on breaks into two halves,
I struggle on my hands and knees,
My face at smoke level.
The roaring fire echoes all around,

All I see now is foggy oranges appearing as
flames to me.
I crouch under cracking wood,
the structure isn't going to hold for much longer,
but I keep trailing onwards.
Smoke trapped inside my lungs,
My eyelids beginning to feel heavy
trying not to close them as I scurry taking every
step.
I see open fields,
the skies ahead, even though things have turned
to night.
I misplace my palm where the smoke lays,
I fall straight ahead,
toppling over on my back,
now stuck in a situation
I don't know exactly how I'm trapped,
but something is blocking my way out,
I push,
With the power I have,
It may just be enough.
BANG.
My entrance suddenly turns dark.
I try to move, but it is near impossible.
I feel the weight of legs on my back.
A horse. A horse that had tumbled right on to
me.
I take a deep breath in,
I won't let the smoke reach my organs,

My back cracks under the pressure,
the horse above is still alive...
but not for long,
and neither will I.

DISTORT

Staring at the alarm clock,
ringing inside my ears.
Time bending the fabric of reality.
Numbers jump like giddy school children,
creating the only light in the room.
It hypnotises,
flashing rhythmically.
I awake from the deep slumber,
Silvia dribbling from my chin.

I turn,
the clock it no longer drums,
my heart feels the motions inside.
Squinting my eyes,
my heart hammers under my chest.
The numbers they dance,
like trees in the wind.
Blinking,
Blinking,
Blinking
Green neon lights running gooey,
crossing from digital and reality.

I peel off the goop,
sticking to my backside,

My fingers,
My nails,
repulsed by the texture.
Long, spindly fingers resemble a witch,
With nails growing twisty,
like vines taking control,
screaming out but no sound is heard.

The carpet, it's also wrapped in goop.
Pulling from the floor,
seeing my tree fingers drop to the ground,
just like magnetic poles.

Crawling back into the covers,
my knees,they squelch.
Scrunching into a tiny ball.
wrapped around me neon green,
like a sea monster.

Beginning to choke,
but then there is just
Silence.
Breathing one mighty breath,
Ripping the sheets from my body.
The goop has vanished into nothingness,
just a fever dream.

Closing eyes tightly,
Rapidly opening them once again.

A strange dark figure,
Staring straight at me.

I blink.
Nothing.
The alarm clicks.
But in the darkness,
a shell of spider,
my own body,
it's flesh,
curled into a pile.
Completely lifeless,
A replica?

Misplaced

Clouds gather,
Neither warm, or chilly,
Pleasant breeze surrounds the air.
Autumn, when trees misplace their leaves.
Crumpled under foot.

The sun, it sets
When children mingle,
for it is Halloween!
The day for the dead.
Confectionery and costumes,
Teenagers hammering,
Drunk and commercialised.
But the dead they sit below,
Awaiting their moment.

He woke from his slumber,
energised, ready.
Sorrowful for the day that it had become.
The smell was putrid.
Torn clothes so rotten,
Years of dirt,
Once black and white suit
Now stained,

with moth bitten nibbles.

Dragging himself up,
digging his claws,
streetlights above came into view.
Perching upon the grave,
Legs dangling,
The tombstone it read:

Dennis Mckee, in memory,
Loving father,
Loving son.

Smile on his face,
But family rarely visited.
Do not dwell not what has been,
For this is an ancient thing.

Something's different,
Things didn't feel right.
His hearing fuzzy,
with no clear message.
His ear!
His ear!
It's detached from the body!
I seemed to have misplaced my ear!

Digging and clawing,

Frantically panicking.
A dead dog in the corner,
Maybe he was the suspect.

Staring at a tree,
growling and barking.
A fleshy ear hanging,
turning and twisting.
Can you catch it?

The dog it pounced,
further up the branches.
Ghost paws and ghost jaws,
Ear wrapped firmly around.
Bouncing down,
ear in mouth,
Fleshy, wet ear was reattached.

Finally, I can hear!

WEB

I met on a dating app,
I couldn't see her face.
Athena? What an unusual name.
A name, it's just a name.
Beautiful! I said.
Hold it!
She forcefully typed.
Are you trying me on?
I panicked,
I scrambled.
No, no no!
Let's start again.
Pause.
Ok.
I asked her how she was.
Not that great, she replied.
Bad luck, it follows me.
What does this mean?
Perhaps too deep?
My arms always open!
Too cheesy?
But weird is good.
My mum, she died,
She began to explain.

This morning.
My dad, he really can't cope.
My own dad died,
I know how it feels.
Things get better,
They have too.
We need to find happiness.
Like the guitar?
You play the guitar?
I'm an artist.
Sculptures.
But here is my work,
just click the link,
look here…

Things don't feel right,
The pauses grow.
Glitching..
GLI..
ITC..
ING…
The sounds they pierce my ears..
TELL ME WHATS GOING ON?

Click the phone.
The phone?
Yes, click it.
Why?
CLICK IT.

Video, it's fuzzy,
The darkness and noise overload my senses.

Hello?

A spider creature,
With legs like sticks,
Crawling from the screen.
Her mother,
covered in blood.
She nestles on the covers,
Teeth like daggers.

What is that?
Caught inside the web,
struggling for freedom.
She's the fly.

Hidden

It's cramped,
But liveable.
Ceiling, sloping down.
Bashing my head above.
Just a circle window,
provides the only light.
My body twisted,
My back bent.

Outside, there's nothing much.
Winter when the snow falls,
tucked up inside.
Freezing temperatures,
All curled up in a pile.

Tiny bed stuffed in a corner,
Walls slopping catching the sheets.
Dry walls, with creaky floors,
I dare not make a squeak.

Feet peeking from below,
With socks full of holes,
Large fur coat,
With scruffy large beard.

Always wishing of food,
Crawling in the dead of night,
Creaking down stairs,
Opening light filled fridges,
An angel in darkness.

Chickens and chocolate cake.
They are such Excellent cooks!
Stashing my pockets,
Full of fruit and veg,
Kneeling on wooden floors,
Food overflowing.

Worrying more often,
Yet sickness isn't the cause.
Painful centre,
Painful back.
No mirror,
No helping hands,
Not knowing what I'm dealt with?

Scared one night,
The Ladders I climbed,
And the food I couldn't touch.
Hungry and worried,
In bed I came back,
Struggling to pull covers.

Such strange event occurred,
Not aware of myself,
Panicking in my mind,
Confronted by a stranger,
hidden in their attic,
Dismissing my existence.

They collected Christmas decorations,
When A terrible thought arose.
You don’t think they had me killed?

Buried

The feeling of sand in my feet.
It sinks in-between my toes.
The beach is always the perfect place to be.
Windows being rolled down,
Wind from the coastline.
A breeze blows my eyes, my hair, taken aback
by its power.
First glimpse of the sea,
Blue, its sparkling.
Sun shines high above, beating on cold waters.
I'm wriggling with excitement,
Should I look through glass or through wind?
Sand dunes move closer,
Sparks of dust flying across tarmac.
Stopped with a HOLT.
Large yellow hills drifting over.

Being patient is the key,
But waiting takes forever.
I dream of running,
I dream of digging.
Where crowds march up,
Deck chairs in hand,
Their children with plastic buckets.
Everyone is trudging,

But I carry on with ease.

Umbrellas are laid,
As father calls out
"Just don't go too far!"
I race to the water,
Dipping each foot,
Its freezing,
And wet.
But better than before.
I must not drink,
I heard myself think.

Friends bound over,
With fascinating objects,
Chatter and conversation lift the senses.

Covering my body,
With the dust and sand.
One patch of sand,
Oddly shaped and bumpy,
Catching the sun's white gleam.

Its white,
Its rough,
It's kind of familiar,
Of course, it is, a bone!
Playing alone,
The fun is too much to handle,

Galloping and bounding
As the family saw.

Faces like ghosts,
Pale as cotton sheets,
Faces dropping like coconuts from a tree.
Something was wrong,
That was obvious to see,
I just didn't know what exactly turned them.

Groups of strangers gathered,
They crowded like sardines,
The Police, they hovered,
I hadn't a clue.
I knew I'd hit jackpot,
As my friends agreed,
Further along the shoreline,
The others happily chewing,
"We've found treasure here!"
"Were eating human bones!"

Exhaust

As humans we blink,
20 times a minute.
Our body motionless,
Muscles out of control.
No time for eyes to stop.
Waking exactly at 3.
Wide opening pupils.
Neither dream nor nightmare.
Feelings of light pushing back.
Staring above,
The shadows dance,
Alive and full of energy.
Gazing at the moon.
Twiddling thumbs.
Falling into a slumber.

That zombie feeling,
Felt every day,
Filling minds with tiredness.
Young people seem full of energy,
Waking before dawn,
It doesn't seem natural,
No not at all.

Gathering around the coffee machine,

The elixir of life,
They huddle and giggle,
Vigour radaring around.
Their nothing much
Seems to be partying all night,
To be invited,
Could make the weak stronger?
Sketchy apartments,
In the dead of night,
Wandering around aimlessly,
Until it's spotted finally.
Handed a bubbling cocktail,
Pink and neon bursting with colour,
A special concoction they said,
Now down the hatch you go

The feeling of power,
The feeling of vivacity,
Gushing around the body
Alive once more.

Dizziness and confusion
Take hold of the soul,
Happiness and Zest
All seem to disappear,
The mind takes over,
The potion takes effect.

One sharp scratch,

Blood gushes around flesh,
The neck its drained,
Weak at the knees,
Their secret to their youth,
Creatures of the night arise.

It's the blood they crave,
Keeping them youthful,
Unable to wake from this nightmare slumber.

Extend

Starting out small,
Leaves, barely any.
No tree, just a twig.
Just covered in grass.
Time passed,
I grew,
Spiney branches,
Gathering its power.
One large oak tree,
I envied most,
Growing for decades,
When I was just a seedling.
Arms grew in every direction,
Standing so proud.
The Wind, it gusts,
She starts on her own,
Spine beefy,
Extendable hands.
She was certain of this world,
I begged to be anything alike.
Moving decades on,
I twisted and turned,
New arms appearing,
Wider trunk,
Bursting through the seams.

Spring had sprung,
I woke refreshed,
Towering over flowers and plants.
Accomplishing my dream,
Basking in the sun rays.
And there she was,
Standing lifeless and still.
Winter had broken her spirit.
Branches turned limp,
The twigs they were broke,
Shaking and falling,
Landing with a
THUMP!
The noise caused an alarm,
She panicked,
Screaming in agony,
Life will come to an end,
Leaving the powerful behind.
I was on top,
Energy sizzling in my leaves.
Feeling the warm summer sun,
Around my trunk below.
Fallen to the ground,
Damped my spirits,
"Don't climb! It's too dangerous!"
Horror had struck,
The feeling hurt me so much.
Pattering's of feet,
Crushing my body,

I couldn’t stand the weight.
I began to realise,
Prettiness isn’t the key,
The power,
The resilience,
She was far more,
A queen,
To the trees.

Catch

Left like a pair of odd socks.
Something is here it shouldn't be.
To be an outsider,
It isn't much of a choice.
First day nerves,
Placed into a category.

Painting, solemnly.
No other decision.
Watching people move,
Legs swinging,
Hands crashing.
Calves touching footballs.

Gazing at the world,
The children wonder.
Like Di Vinci in Italy,
Less finesse.
A genius at work,
Not that I'm comparing.

Football is such a messy game,
Dirt being spilled,
Swollen feet and grubby toes.

Sheltered away,
Under a willow tree,
Sketchbook in hand.
Understand how legs worked,
Sketching the movement
Just like a machine.
The sudden bristle of something on my ankle.

Beefy and tall,
A figure rose above me.
Apologises were given.
Seems I was miles away.
Insisting I could throw back over,
He left with a humph,
Why had I inconvenienced him so?

Maths.
Creativity seemed to vanish.
Tip tap toe on my shoulder.
Spinning around,
Loser!
Not strong enough for me?
Morning once more,
He stood staring.
What was his problem?
CATCH THIS.
I heard a yell.
Object flying through the skies.
The ground I hit, with a large

BUMP.

Crowds gathered in shock.
Being scooped from,
Taken away.
One last smirk he left.

Checked for bruises,
None were found.
I scribbled on paper,
A silly revenge fantasy.
He lay their crying,
Large balls of metal spiralling out of control.
I felt the fire burning inside me,
Pencil stroking paper.

CATCH!
The words scribbled to side.
I sniggered,
I jeered
At what I had created
Only to see a boy
Covered in scratches,
Severely injured.

A strange event occurred,
Just sitting he was,
Flying in the air,
Nobody behind.

The boys' eyes flickered,
Head twisting around,
"You told me to catch."

Breathe

We breathe.
We take for granted.
Our Lungs,
We take for granted,
Like we don't care.
Freezing mornings,
Dreaded Christmas shopping begun,
Crowded and pushed,
Sounds like my idea of hell.
Parked, squished next to trash,
I'm just one part of this mad rush.
Thrusted and shoved,
Piles toppled on each other.
I'm old, but not frail,
Weaker, but still hold my own.
Head screwed on,
Tunnel vision.
Knowing exactly what to do.
The warmth rises,
With so many bodies,
Eyes focused on the end in sight.
The light is there,
Just a few meters ahead,
A wall of flesh,
Grinding to a holt.

Commotion and panic.
Spreads through rising heat.
Too dangerous to let us go,
They say the air is infected.
From the view outside,
Strangers struggle for breath,
Dying like wasps in Fall.
Crushing into walls,
Individuals hurled outside,
There's not much hope now,
Breathe in, or breathe out.

Bite

A bite of Satan's fruit.
Not like any fairytale.
No voluptuous taste.
Juices pouring down.
Gracefully landing on the ground.
No sweet old lady.
No gentle touch.

Grabbed by the neck.
Hair pulled by force.
Stale, old toilet water.
Being forced inside.

A man's voice bellowing.
Deciding fate.
Rotten fruit.
Touching lips.
Tingling.
Foul smelling.

The only view of feet.
Pressed against a wall.
Teeth digging.
Teeth crunching.
Black slimy maggots.

A non happy ending.
Which started this mess.
Not stuck in miserable lives.
Clinging for hope.

Money makes the world go round.
Life become dry.
A deal was made.
For an excellent opportunity.
A good fortune.
Bathing in riches.
More time for parties.

More insanity.
More expense.
Frivolously spending.
No care for the outcome.

A joke.
A jeer.
The deal not real.
Spending.
Gorging.
Things not there.
A fool.
They laughed and bellowed.
The fruit sliding down flesh.
You should have seen your face.

Stranger

I write this journal,
Starting a new life.
Away from foggy fumes of the city.
A flower business I shall start,
Away from it all.
New people,
New faces to meet.
Rolling hills,
Beautiful vista.
The sights and smells filling the senses.

I'm like an ugly duckling,
In the midst of all the swans.
No welcome messages,
No happy greetings,
Feeling lost,
Without a place.

Entering the bar,
With squeaky floor boards.
Burning fires,
Seeming so inviting.
Sitting by my lonesome,
No one wants to share.

I'm stuck in world now where no one seems to care.

Luck may have it,
Fate seemed to change,
Strangers, new friends,
Wanting to know me better.
A summoning,
An invitation,
A chance to know them better.

A nasty surprise was left that night,
Spread upon my shop wall,
YOU DON'T BELONG,
GO BACK HOME.
Shakes me to the core.

HELP, ME PLEASE.
EVERYTHING'S GONE CRAZY.
Trapped and frightened,
No way of returning.

Panicked and horrified,
I'm in danger, I know that well,
They want to BURN ME,
To snuff me into hell.
There's no nice way to say this,
I was prey for them it seems,
That death for me is shortly going to come.

DIG

Feeling some squelch,
Mud covering the area,
Hair.
Boots.
Drenched in dirt.
Arising to the ground,
Luckily alone.

The same trail was walked.
Near forests and nature.
To clear the mind.
Leaves sprinkled.
Crunching underfoot.

Taking the route,
Along the path ahead,
A nudge was felt.
Feet incased.
Crumpled paper,
Lay hidden,
Feet squeezing.

Writing was scrunched.
The ink splattered.
The remanence of a map.
Perhaps a child's sketch,

A practical joke?

Further investigation,
The more professional it seemed.
X MARKS THE SPOT.
In minuscule letting.

Nearer,
Nearer,
The path dragged on.
A mound of earth unlike the others.
DO NOT DIG
The sign it read,
No way anyway,
No shovel to be found.

It may be madness,
digging with bare hands?
Desperate urge,
Curiosity beckons.

Dig,
Dig.
Human claw marks appeared,
Crouched on hands and knees.
No treasure to be found.

But There ahead,
a shovel sat patiently,

Grabbing with en vigueur.
DIG
DIG
DIG
Once more,
Until the sun began closing its eyes.

The night had arrived,
No longer was it safe outside.
Like a creature,
The feeling inside,
Continued to push.

Inside the mound,
Parts of things that were found,
Dragging until..
Flesh.
Dried.
Human.
Flesh.

More tugging,
More shoving,
Full of desperation,
A large force of nature.
A body in full.
Like staring into a mirror.

Hold

So miniature.
With tiny fingers,
With tiny mouth,
And tiny ears.
A lost lamb in headlights.
Warm to touch.
Pink ball of skin,
Eyes welling up.
Water droplets bouncing.
Close to the chest,
Heat radiates,
Locking stares,
Feeling a connection.
The pain inside.
The face seems familiar,
Like mature cheddar.
Growing like fine red wine.
Pupils they shrunk,
Gripping tighter-to the breast.
Holding on,
Until they could not cling any longer.
Once the size of dinner plate,
Now human sized.
Small tufted scalp,
long strands of hair.

No other choice,
Arms now outstretched.
A living,
Breathing,
Soul.
Gazed over.
Looking terrified.
Pupils they dilated,
Lips cracking,
Legs like violin strings.
Towering over,
6ft it seemed,
Peering down in sorrow.
They felt apologetic,
Watching my shadow shrink.
Weak, less powerful.
I started to sense.
Bones crumbling,
Falling like rocks.
A bent posture,
As a flamingo would stand.
Palm of my hands,
Wrinkled like paper.
Legs and arms flapping.
They stared back like a mirror,
Kneeling before me,
Holding the body tightly,
The head against the chest.
Power in they're muscles,

Stood out against my flesh,
Breaking apart at any moment.
When they did,
I drifted from the ether,
Skin flaking.
There in front,
They began the same process,
skin loosing up,
Panic behind the eyes,
Before calm washed us over.
Both decaying,
But at separate times,
No longer sadness hidden.
Our shaken, paper hands,
Stretching out,
Weakness.
But Happiness.
Grabbing to our bodies.
Turned to dust,
before they're eyes,
The presence is felt all around.
I watch,
Seeing myself at peace,
Ashes one moment,
Gone the next.
Darkness infects the soul.
Peering through my eyelids,
Welcomed by reality.
With age we grow slowly,

There was no baby,
Still I pressed pressure on my chest.
For this was my reality.

www.ingramcontent.com/pod-product-compliance
Lightning Source LLC
Chambersburg PA
CBHW051736130826
49812CB00033B/890
9789357210560